W9-AKX-393

CCSS **Genre** Expository Text

Essential Question
Why are natural resources valuable?

The Delta

BY JAMES MCNAUGHTON

Introduction

The mighty Mississippi River is famous throughout the world. It is the largest river in North America, and over many years, it has created an extraordinary region called the Mississippi Delta.

A delta usually refers to land that has been built up by **sediment** at the mouth of a river, but the Mississippi Delta is much bigger. This vast region is an alluvial plain, created by flooding across parts of seven states. It covers more than 3 million acres, stretching from southern Illinois all the way to the Gulf of Mexico.

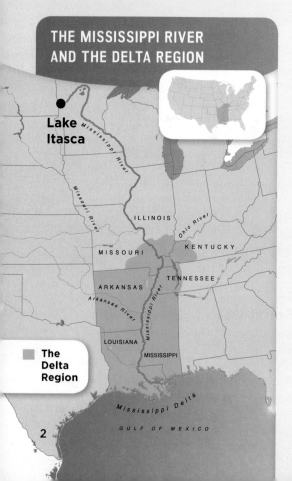

THE MISSISSIPPI RIVER AND THE DELTA REGION

Lake Itasca

Mississippi River

Missouri River

ILLINOIS

Ohio River

MISSOURI

KENTUCKY

ARKANSAS

TENNESSEE

Arkansas River

Mississippi River

LOUISIANA

MISSISSIPPI

The Delta Region

Mississippi Delta

GULF OF MEXICO

The Delta region has abundant **natural resources**. Food is grown on its **fertile** floodplains, and its oil and natural gas provide **domestic** sources of energy.

Many of the Delta region's products are transported on the Mississippi River. The river is like a huge, watery highway. It connects all of the region's towns and cities and provides access to the Gulf of Mexico.

The Delta region has magnificent wilderness areas too. Its **ecosystems** support diverse populations of plants, birds, fish, and other animals.

Powering this wealth of natural resources is, of course, water. It was water that created this landscape from the beginning, and water continues to be the region's biggest feature. Today issues of water quality and control are vital to the future of the Delta region.

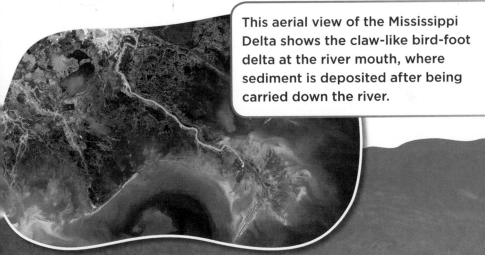

This aerial view of the Mississippi Delta shows the claw-like bird-foot delta at the river mouth, where sediment is deposited after being carried down the river.

RIVER PLAINS AND DELTAS

As rivers flow from their upper to their lower reaches, they pick up and carry small stones and silt. This material is called alluvium, or sediment. Alluvium is carried along the river and eventually deposited somewhere. Over time, with repeated floods, the sediment spreads out and creates land. Often this land forms a delta area around the river mouth, but the Mississippi Delta's giant alluvial plain extends far inland as well.

In the lower part of the Mississippi Delta, where the fresh water of the river meets seawater in the Gulf of Mexico, the river slows down and releases even more sediment. Here at the river mouth, sediment has gradually built up on both sides of the river channel in a claw-like shape called a bird-foot delta.

CHAPTER 1
The Power of Water

The Mississippi is one of the world's great rivers. It is about 2,300 miles (3,700 kilometers) long. Its exact length is hard to measure because the river is always changing. The river's source is Lake Itasca, in Itasca State Park, Minnesota. Many scientists believe this lake was carved out by glaciers thousands of years ago during the Great Ice Age. It takes three months for a drop of water to travel all the way from the river's source to its mouth in the Gulf of Mexico!

The Mississippi River and Delta region have always been a rich resource. Native Americans benefited from the region's mild climate and fertile soil. They cultivated maize and depended on the river for fish, transportation, and trade.

Today, the Delta is a nationally important region for agriculture, industry, and energy production. All of these resources and activities depend on the availability of water.

The Mississippi River contributes to the entire country's economic and environmental well-being.

The powerful Mississippi River carries a massive amount of water. In some places, it **discharges** about 600,000 cubic feet of water per second. However, the river behaves differently all the time; it is an ever-changing force. As the water flows in the river and its many **tributaries**, it varies in depth, speed, and even color!

Some water from the Mississippi takes on a different form altogether, evaporating and condensing to become rain or snow. During times of heavy rainfall or snowmelt, the volume of water in the river swells and the river overflows, flooding large tracts of land. This is another part of the natural water cycle.

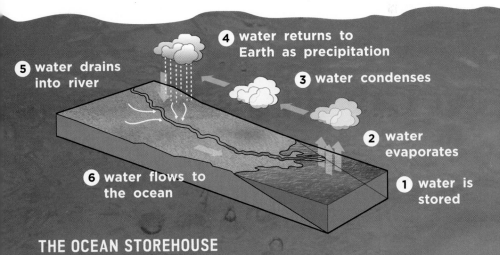

4 water returns to Earth as precipitation

5 water drains into river

3 water condenses

2 water evaporates

6 water flows to the ocean

1 water is stored

THE OCEAN STOREHOUSE

In the water cycle, water circulates constantly between Earth and the atmosphere. Oceans store nearly 97 percent of Earth's water, some of which returns to the atmosphere as evaporation. The evaporated water condenses in clouds and falls as rain or snow onto land and into lakes, streams and rivers, and even back into the ocean.

The rainwater that drains from the land and collects in the Mississippi River flows back into the Gulf of Mexico and eventually will evaporate once more. The water cycle just keeps repeating!

While floods can be a challenge for people in the Delta region, it is flooding that has made the region's soil so fertile. Floodwaters carry nutrient-rich sediment that acts as a natural fertilizer. This renews the topsoil, so crops flourish. The soil is also enriched by the Delta's **diversity** of plant life. When plants die, the soil absorbs their nutrients and recycles their energy.

Along with fertile soil and abundant water, the region's temperate climate is also an advantage for agriculture. Warm temperatures make growing conditions ideal all year long. More than half of the Delta region's land area is used for agriculture. Most of the country's soybeans, rice, sugar cane, feed grains, hay, and cotton are grown here.

In the past, cotton crops created fortunes for plantation owners in the southern states. Cotton remains an important crop for the region today.

The region's forests also make a significant contribution to the Delta region's economy. The timber industry developed before the Civil War and peaked in the late 1800s. However, the number of hardwood forests was declining by the early 1900s.

Today, forestry is managed in a more **sustainable** way. Most of the timber is used for lumber, and about 30 percent of it is used as pulp for making paper.

Throughout the history of the timber industry, the river has provided a fast and efficient method for transporting logs.

CHAPTER 2

The River's Bounty

The Mississippi Delta is an important region for the nation's energy supply. The Delta has large quantities of **fossil fuels**, including oil, or petroleum, and natural gas. Oil and gas form slowly over millions of years when the remains of tiny warm-water plants and animals are buried in the seabed and compressed under high pressure.

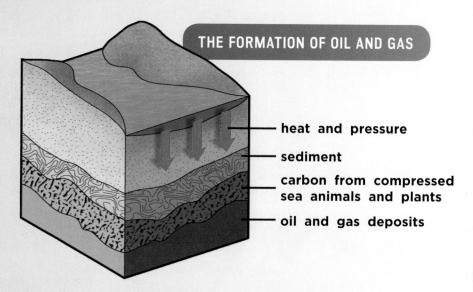

THE FORMATION OF OIL AND GAS

- heat and pressure
- sediment
- carbon from compressed sea animals and plants
- oil and gas deposits

The petroleum industry began in the region in the early 1900s. While supplies are now declining, the Delta region still produces about 200,000 barrels of oil a year. Offshore oil rigs in the Gulf of Mexico also provide oil and gas resources.

The Delta benefits from the petrochemical manufacturing plants and other crucial industries in the region, but these activities can also pose risks for the natural environment.

Oil and gas development has helped the economy. However, it can damage the Delta's ecosystems. Pipelines that transport oil and gas through wetland areas to storage facilities may disrupt natural water cycles. Oil can seep out from cracks in pipes.

In addition, the region is vulnerable to large oil spills from offshore oil rigs located in the Gulf. In 2010, oil from the Deepwater Horizon spill washed onto the Delta's coastline around Louisiana and Mississippi. The impact of this spill made headlines around the world.

The Delta region also provides mineral resources, including iron, sand, clay, marble, and limestone. The profits from these minerals are not as substantial as the profits from oil and gas. However, they are still an important source of jobs and income for the area. Most mineral resources are used locally and transported much shorter distances, leaving a smaller **carbon footprint**.

The Mississippi River carries about half of the nation's inland water cargo. This amounts to nearly 500 million tons every year! Cargo is transported either by barges guided by tugboats, or by ships, depending on how deep the river is. The Mississippi connects to other major rivers, such as the Ohio and Missouri rivers, and with the Gulf of Mexico. New Orleans, on the Gulf, is one of the world's busiest ports.

The Mississippi River is one of the world's biggest and busiest waterways.

Tourism and recreation are other vital industries for the Delta. They provide hundreds of thousands of jobs and billions of dollars in revenue. Millions of people visit each year, attracted by the region's rich history and culture, as well as by its landscapes.

The Delta region also supports one of the most diverse and profitable fisheries in the world. Among the fish sold commercially are catfish, buffalo fish, spoonbill fish, and garfish. However, the region's freshwater fish populations are shrinking due to reduced habitats and the effects of pollution.

CHAPTER 3

Protecting the Delta

The Delta region's ecosystems include large forested wetlands and lowland hardwood forests. These areas are home to a great diversity of animal species.

The Mississippi Delta's forested wetlands are particularly important to the region's ecology. Scientists estimate that less than 30 percent of the Delta's forested wetlands remain. Agriculture, forestry, energy development, and water-control projects have all contributed to the loss of wetland areas.

Wetlands may seem like dull, muddy places to some people, but they are vital in many ways. They are a habitat for many species of birds and fish. The wetlands provide them with food, shelter, and safe places to breed. Wetlands prevent sediment from being washed out to sea. They act as a buffer against incoming storms, reducing **erosion**. They also affect water quality by filtering out pollutants and helping keep the water clean.

The heron is one native species that lives in the Delta wetlands.

The Mississippi River is also a globally important flyway. Birds fly above it when they migrate between North and South America. About 8 million ducks, geese, swans, and other waterbirds are estimated to breed and spend the winter in the region's wetlands.

MISSISSIPPI FLYWAY

CANADA

KEY
—— Mississippi River
▬▬ Main flyway paths

N
W—E
S

MEXICO

Over 180 different species of freshwater fish live in the region's waters. Other animal species native to the Delta include black bears, deer, mink, otters, alligators, and turtles. Bald eagles and peregrine falcons also live there. Some of these animals are endangered.

Water is essential for all living things. The health of the Delta region's ecosystems relies on the cleanliness of the water in the river. Chemical runoff from factories and farms can pollute the water. Sewage and wastewater from cities and towns can foul it, too.

Levees and dams have been built to control water in the Mississippi Delta. These can disrupt the cycles that created the region. A delta needs regular deposits of sediment to survive. However, sediment from the Mississippi is being either trapped upriver or dumped far out at sea instead of building up the land.

Scientists believe that over time, between 50 and 70 percent of the Mississippi's sediment has been prevented from reaching the lower parts of the Delta. As a result, the region's coastline is gradually submerging. If nothing is done, an area nearly the size of Connecticut could disappear by the end of the century.

Water control projects such as this dam have reduced flooding and saved many lives, but they have also greatly reduced the amount of sediment that is carried down the river.

WATER CONTROL

There are many forms of water control in the Mississippi Delta. In the past, dredging was often carried out to make water channels deeper and to create new waterways. Dams provide water for irrigation systems that were built to allow crops to be grown during times of drought. Dams and levees also limit damage from flooding. There are about 8,000 dams in the Mississippi River system and more than 30,000 levees.

Today more people are aware of the necessity of protecting and conserving the region's environment. Many people are dedicated to helping clean up the Delta. Efforts range from local conservation projects by individual landowners and groups to new laws and regulations by state and federal governments.

Scientists and engineers are working on large-scale plans to restore the coastal areas of the Delta. Their challenge is to stop the land from eroding without disrupting shipping. These plans focus on diverting the river—this time to cause, rather than prevent, flooding. New sediment from these forced floods can then build up in the shallow coastal water, creating new delta land.

PREDICTED MISSISSIPPI DELTA COASTLINE

Baton Rouge

Mississippi River

Lafayette

New Orleans

KEY

Coastline today

Predicted coastline in 100 years

Scientists are forecasting that rising seas and loss of sediment could drastically reduce the remaining amount of coastal delta land by 2100 if erosion continues at its present rate. They are working on plans to prevent this from happening.

Other projects focus on restoring forested wetlands. Still others aim to get rid of introduced exotic species that have overrun native species. These projects save threatened wildlife from extinction and also improve water quality.

Many people are looking for ways to make the region's industry and agriculture more sustainable. New measures, or rules, have been introduced to conserve water. Others aim to reduce the pollution caused by chemical runoff from farming and industry.

Many different groups and individuals are involved in conservation projects in the Delta region.

Conclusion

The Mississippi Delta region is like a natural powerhouse for the nation. It supplies a wealth of natural resources upon which people throughout the United States depend. In the past, the region's resources were exploited without thought for the future. The Delta's vast size had encouraged people to think that its assets had no limits.

Today, more people realize that the Delta ecosystems are fragile. Their natural cycles need to be protected. The oil and gas will eventually run out. However, the river and the Delta are sustainable and can be preserved.

Water is the lifeblood of the Delta. The focus on harnessing the Delta's wealth has shifted now to conserving water and restoring the region's natural cycles.

Human activity is a critical part of the Delta's cycles. Both agriculture and industry are interconnected with the region's ecosystems. People are introducing new methods of farming and irrigation. Better technologies for mineral, oil, and gas extraction are helping to prevent further damage to the environment. The region's future depends on making all of these activities work for the benefit of its environment, economy, and people.

Different organizations are also joining forces to solve the Delta's problems. Partnerships are being formed in the region to harness the energy and ideas of as many people as possible, from school students to landowners to politicians.

It is only by learning from the mistakes of the past that we may be able to restore and safeguard the health of the Mississippi Delta for the future.

By preserving the Delta environment and its many wildlife species, we can ensure that its resources are protected for the future.

Respond to Reading

Summarize

Use the most important details from *The Delta* to summarize what you learned about the Delta region. Your graphic organizer may help you.

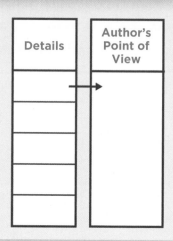

Details	Author's Point of View

Text Evidence

1. How do you know that *The Delta* is an expository text? Give examples of text features. **GENRE**

2. What is the author's point of view about protecting the Mississippi Delta? Give examples from the text that support his position. **AUTHOR'S POINT OF VIEW**

3. What does the word *alluvium* on page 3 mean? What information in the text helped you define the word? **DEFINITIONS AND RESTATEMENTS**

4. Write about the author's point of view about the Mississippi Delta in Chapter 1. Give facts and examples the author uses to express his point of view. **WRITE ABOUT READING**

Compare Texts
Read about how waste can be used to make
a valuable resource.

Get Rich with Compost

To grow well, plants need soil that is rich in nutrients. In nature, soil may be enriched in a number of ways. When rivers flood land, as they do in the Mississippi Delta region, they leave behind mineral-rich sediment. Volcanic material, such as lava, is also very rich in minerals. With sufficient rainfall, it breaks down very quickly. Over time, this material makes some of the most fertile soil on Earth.

Plants themselves are a very important source of nutrients. When they die, they decompose and release their nutrients back into the soil so other plants can use them. This natural cycle is self-sustaining.

When a tree's leaves decompose into leaf mold, their nutrients can be absorbed by the tree's roots. This allows their energy to be recycled.

You don't need a river or volcano in your backyard to create soil that is rich in nutrients. All you need to do is create a compost bin to recycle your household food scraps and plant waste such as yard trimmings. These will decompose into mulch, which is rich in nutrients and is a great organic fertilizer for the garden.

By composting, you are creating your own natural cycle. Your garden plants will be healthier, you won't need to buy other fertilizers, and you'll have less trash to throw away. It's a win–win solution!

It's best to begin composting when the weather is warm because the waste will decay more quickly. You can buy a compost bin that is ready to assemble and use or you can make one from spare timber and other materials. You can even just build a compost heap. Compost is usually made outdoors, but a special type of bin can be used to make it indoors.

There are a variety of approaches to composting. Usually the compost should be kept moist with water and turned occasionally to allow air to circulate through it. It should have equal amounts of "brown" material (dead leaves, twigs, branches) and "green" material (fruit and vegetable scraps, coffee grounds, grass clippings). Ask a local gardener or garden store for advice about what works best in your area.

Compost can be used as a growing medium for outdoor plants or spread under shrubs and on garden beds. It saves money and resources and helps plants thrive.

The Dos and Don'ts of Composting

	✔ What to Compost	✘ What Not to Compost
food	fruits and vegetables; coffee grounds; teabags; eggshells	dairy products; food scraps such as meat and fish bones
paper	shredded paper	glossy paper
clothing	cotton and wool fabrics	polyester and nylon
household trash	dryer and vacuum-cleaner lint; wood ashes; sawdust and wood chips	coal or charcoal ashes
plants	house plants; leaves and yard clippings	diseased plants; yard trimmings treated with chemical pesticides

Make Connections

How does making compost help conserve natural resources? **ESSENTIAL QUESTION**

Compare the natural fertilizers present in the Mississippi Delta with the fertilizers produced by making compost. **TEXT TO TEXT**

Glossary

carbon footprint *(KAHR-buhn FOOT-print)* the impact on the environment of carrying goods from one place to another *(page 9)*

discharges *(dis-CHAHRJ-iz)* moves water through the river *(page 5)*

diversity *(duh-VUHR-suh-tee)* having many different types or species *(page 6)*

domestic *(duh-MES-tik)* within the United States *(page 2)*

ecosystems *(EE-koh-sis-tuhmz)* communities of plants and animals within a habitat *(page 3)*

erosion *(i-ROH-zhuhn)* carrying away by natural forces, such as water or wind *(page 11)*

fertile *(FUHR-tuhl)* able to produce a lot of vegetation or crops *(page 2)*

fossil fuels *(FAH-suhl fyewlz)* fuels formed from plant and animal remains buried long ago *(page 8)*

levees *(LE-veez)* raised banks of channels *(page 13)*

natural resources *(NA-chuh-ruhl REE-sawrs-iz)* things found in nature that can be used by humans *(page 2)*

sediment *(SE-duh-muhnt)* material such as sand that is deposited by rivers or the wind *(page 2)*

sustainable *(suh-STAY-nuh-buhl)* done in a way that does not damage the environment *(page 7)*

tributaries *(TRI-byuh-ter-eez)* divisions or branches of a river *(page 5)*

Index

Focus on Science

Purpose To see how pollutants enter the watershed through runoff

Procedure

Step 1 Work with a partner or in a small group. Take a sheet of paper, crumple it up, and then smooth out the paper a little bit. Leave some big creases, so it has high points and low points. The paper represents the land, or watershed, near the Mississippi River.

Step 2 Use two to three different colors of washable marker. Trace over the paper creases, or folds, with marker. Use more than one color in some creases. The markers represent pollutants such as fertilizer and other chemicals or waste.

Step 3 Put your crumpled paper into a shallow pan or tray. Fill a spray bottle with clean water and spray the paper with the water. Observe what happens.

Conclusion Describe what happened at the highest and lowest points in the watershed. Did the different pollutants mix together? What do you think the water from the spray bottle represents? What does the water in the tray represent? How does this experiment connect to what you read about in *The Delta*?